BELOVED HOMES!

A drop-in book of nine much-loved homes, from those of us who love life at home

WELL WE'VE
HAD A FANTASTIC
TIME!

In the spring and summer, we at IKEA FAMILY paid a visit to nine families all over Sweden. The result is a very personal book that reflects the way Swedes furnish their homes – something IKEA has had a little influence on over the years, of course.

We haven't made a statistical selection of the average Swedish family, but instead we've taken a look at the different lives of nine different families. One couple lives in a magnificent 18th century mansion, while another family with two children lives in a small, but smart, house.

The one thing that all the nine families have in common is quite simple. They love their homes. And we love them, because they've invited us into their lives and let us take photos and talk about their homes. Thanks! What we'd really like to do is take a look inside your home, and all the family homes of every size, all over the world. Families in houses and apartments. Families with kids, with no kids, with a dog, or a lizard, families with tons of stuff and families with hardly any stuff at all. But of course that just isn't possible. This time.

WELCOME INSIDE!

Lena Allblom
Project Manager
IKEA FAMILY

BELOVED
FISKARGRÄND

In a stuccoed house from the 1920s, just outside the city,

lives a family of two adults, a boy of five and a little baby.

The house is on two floors and has a basement, and because they need

all the space they can get, the basement is furnished.

They're also about to convert the attic into a children's bedroom.

And this family loves their home.

Step inside, have a look around and find out why.

8   Here we have a living room with a generous sofa and rug, both white. But is that a good idea for a family with young children? Absolutely –
if the cover is removable and machine washable it's ideal, because after a quick wash even the sofa of a family with children can look fresh,

clean and white like new. And while they're doing the laundry anyway, they might as well throw in that cotton rug.

in a family like this, life is easier if the kids are allowed in any room. that way, you don't spend your time chasing them around telling them where they can't go. here there's always room for the children. the living room is just as much for playing as it is for resting and relaxing. and there are smart storage solutions all over the house to make sure there's room for all those fun things.

The living room is adjacent to the kitchen, and both rooms have the same blinds that filter and disperse the daylight.

A large wall cabinet can take the kids' toys as well as mom and dad's important stuff.

a shelf behind the sofa gives them an exciting, flexible space where they can display a few beautiful things. there's also room for lighting, either for reading or creating atmosphere. and rather than hanging up the pictures, they've leaned them against the wall. if they get tired of one masterpiece they can swap it without worrying about hooks or holes in the wall.

Three different storage solutions, strikingly beautiful.

Here all the CDs, DVDs and videos are kept out of the children's reach, so mom and dad can keep an eye on the family's consumption of home entertainment.

13

14   In this home, many a happy hour is spent in the basement. There's a workroom, a bathroom and a large, practical laundry room with plenty of space for field hockey. Field hockey? Well, if there isn't enough room to run around in the rest of the house, the basement makes a perfect gymnasium.

15

in the laundry room there's a long countertop for sorting and folding laundry, a washing machine, dryer and clothesline, a large shower, plenty of open and closed storage, and even a little bit of daylight.

USUAL COMMENT FROM GUESTS:
"WHY DON'T YOU COVER UP THOSE UGLY FUSE BOXES? AT LEAST PUT A SHEET OVER THEM SO IT LOOKS MORE PRESENTABLE."

USUAL ANSWER:
"WHY? A BASEMENT SHOULD LOOK LIKE ONE."

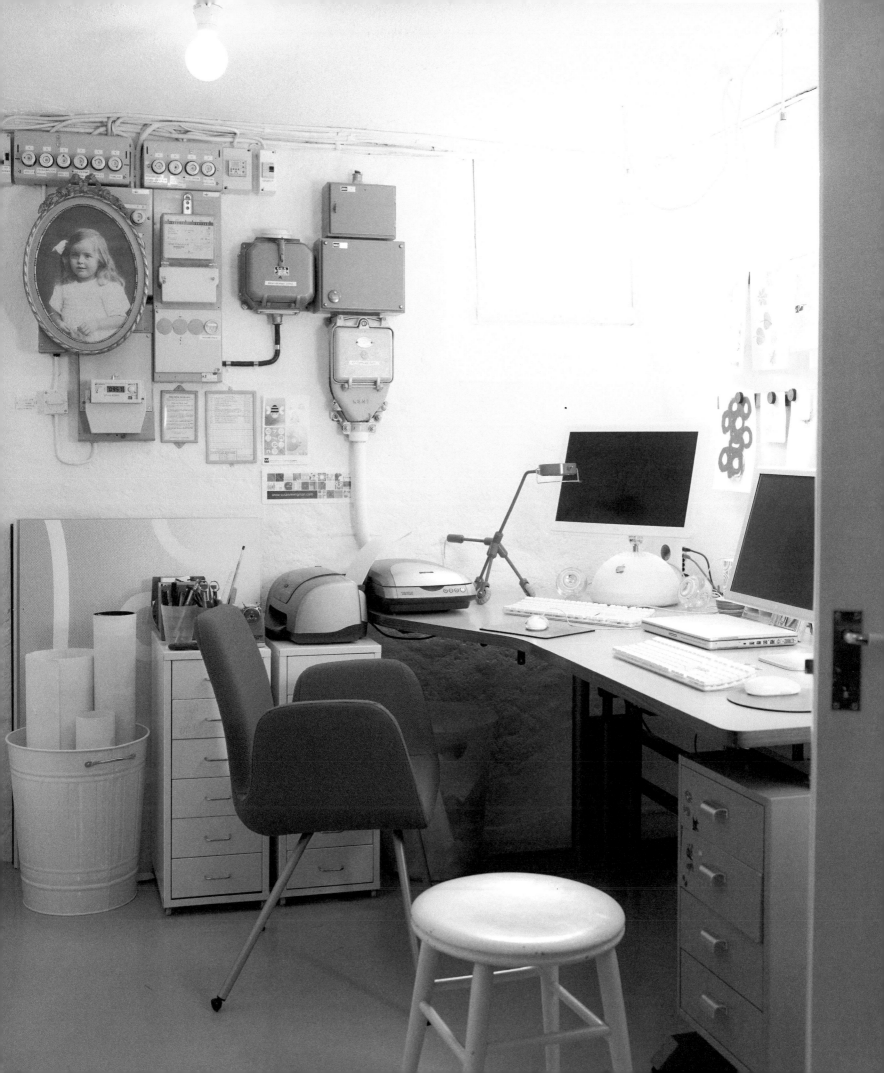

20 When the kitchen cabinets are simple and well-planned like this, with the same width on the wall and base cabinets, you can afford to go all out with a colorful, practical wax tablecloth and kitchen chairs in different styles and colors.

Here the everyday junk has its own cabinet that can fit quite a lot of keys, cell phones and modeling clay. The shelves above it are for favorite things and everyday cookbooks. An attractive eye-catcher that also serves a function.

22   The smart parent with young children naturally adds an extra range to make cooking more efficient.

IT'S NOT ONLY WE HUMANS WHO LIKE BEING IN THE KITCHEN.

all kinds of other things gravitate to it too. phones, bills, handbags, reminders from the dentist and other everyday stuff. but maybe it's not so strange. after all, the kitchen is the heart of a home, and maybe all those scraps of paper and sunglasses can feel that. they want to be where it's happening too. but with good closed storage behind the table, the kitchen is a clutter-free zone.

A must in any hall: the not-slip-when-put-ting-your-shoes-on stool and a thick mat that absorbs the worst of the undershoe dirt.

IF THE HALL'S A BIT TIGHT, MAKE IT BIGGER BY BUILDING IN SOME AIR AND LIGHT. HERE, THE GLASS WALL SOFTENS THE LOOK AND BRINGS IN INDIRECT SUNLIGHT FROM THE LIVING ROOM. AND THE CLOTHES RACK IS DELIBERATELY PLACED SLIGHTLY HIGHER SO AIR AND LIGHT CAN CIRCULATE BETWEEN THE CLOTHES AND SHOES.

The wardrobe door has been replaced by a fabric curtain to bring softness and color to the room. With textiles you can be a bit braver with colors because they're so easy to change.

useful stuff when you're five:
a big, sturdy red play table, a sturdy rug that doesn't slide around on the floor, a sturdy bedside lamp, a sturdy wall to hang your pictures on.

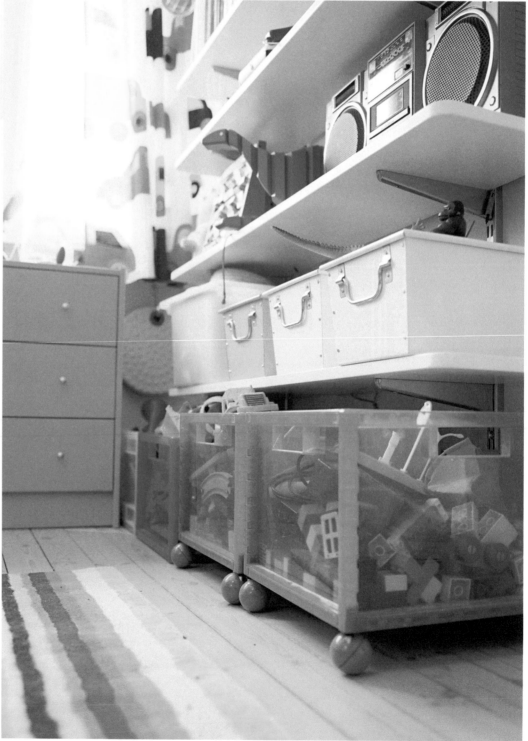

Almost all five-year-olds have an unlimited need for storage. Both open and closed. For things they use a lot, and some of the things that make only a rare appearance. And this five-year-old is no exception. Boring stuff, like clothes, is in the lower drawer. And all the important things like toy figures, Lego, dinosaurs, building blocks, knight's costumes, balls, dolls and crayons are close at hand in boxes and storage crates. And the wall-mounted shelving can swallow a whole lot.

A bedside table each, a bedside lamp each and a shared bed. A good basic package for any bedroom. This room also has some extras: a lovely fabric headboard and a small children's bed at the foot for night-wandering children to sleep in.

the top three for a nursing mother and her hungry baby: a comfortable nursing chair with washable cover, a crib close to a drop of daylight and a changing table with plenty of storage. and to help big brother watch when it's diaper-changing time - a stool to stand on.

BYE-BYE FROM US ON FISKARGRÄND!

BELOVED
HÖGHULT

Mom, dad and their 10-year-old twin girls left the city to live in the country.

Close to nature. Close to all the animals. A place where they could find

some peace and quiet. But the peace and quiet soon went out

the window when all their friends came to visit, weekend after weekend.

In fact this hospitality marathon is probably going on right now, in

the stunning wilds of southern Sweden. Just follow the laughter far,

far into the forest and you'll see a 17th century log house with

a guest cottage, playhouse and carpenter's workshop.

And a barn for partying.

The nice thing about really old houses is that the best solution is the simplest one — not the most expensive one. In this country kitchen the family moved the dining table out to make room for a large, freestanding island ideal for food preparation. Now they have a generous

countertop that also provides a lot of storage. Behind the countertop, 20 metal boxes (thankfully labeled) create a kind of "box pantry."

the man of the house was reluctant to part with his wood-burning stove:
"it actually heats up the entire ground floor and is perfect for cooking."
and of course the lady of the house couldn't live without a new gas stove:
"fine, but i'm not cooking on it, i want a fast gas stove!"
the family crisis was resolved by a local blacksmith who linked the stoves together with an enormous hood.

BLACK! ARE YOU OUT OF YOUR MIND?

THE VAST MAJORITY OF SWEDISH HOMES ARE LIGHT. LIGHT WALLS, LIGHT FLOORS. AND MAYBE IT'S NOT SO STRANGE THAT WE CHOOSE LIGHT COLORS, SINCE WE SCANDINAVIANS NEED ALL THE LIGHT WE CAN GET – AFTER ALL, THE WINTER AND FALL ARE DARK SEASONS HERE, WITHOUT MUCH DAYLIGHT. THAT'S WHY A BLACK WALL CREATES SUCH AN IMPACT IN THESE LIGHT HOMES. TRY PAINTING ONE WALL BLACK AND YOU'LL DISCOVER IT MAKES THE LIGHT LOOK EVEN LIGHTER.

40   Last time they counted, they had 14 folding party tables and 68 spindle-back chairs.

WOW,
THEY LOVE THEIR HOME!
AND WOW,
DO THEY KNOW HOW TO
THROW A PARTY!

The twins are moving up a grade in school
– let's have a party!
Dad's fixed the fence
– that's worth celebrating!
Mom's bought 60 linen towels at a
flea market
– let's invite 60 people over for dinner!
Mom's bought 40 chairs
– set the table again!

Really mom!
Another flea market?
60 pressed-glass side plates at
10 cents each?

42   The dining table that was moved out of the kitchen ended up here. And it's a pretty nice place, because this is where everyone comes to do absolutely everything. Renovate chairs, eat breakfast, lunch and dinner, do jigsaw puzzles, dance, paint, tease one another, sit and chat over a cup of coffee and

play cards. Look at the picture carefully and you'll see two drop-leaf tables, probably 14 chairs ingeniously hidden along the walls à la 18th century, wicker chairs that can be pulled right up to the table. See how everything's ready for a massive party but you don't really notice it?

the key to keeping this swedish country house from looking too "cottagey" is not to use too much furniture. that way, the architecture acts as a kind of furniture in itself.

All the outdoor toys are concealed under the bench seat in the hall. Dirty hockey sticks, 500 balls (mom at the flea market again?) jump ropes, lawn games and a few lost or forgotten gloves.

48   Having the hanging-rail extend the length of the whole wall and carrying it on the other side of the door makes it feel extra genuine and natural. The rail also gives a good sense of the family makeup, with a mix of pajamas, overalls, second-hand dresses and hand-knitted clothes.

everything you need for a
cozy bedroom: raw, chilly
weather, an open fireplace
for warming feet and hearts,
and breakfast in bed, until
lunch with the whole family
and a really thick newspaper.

Unfortunately, size standardization hadn't been invented in the 1600s, so normal wardrobes were out of the question here — the ceiling wasn't high enough. What you can do though is go to a flea market (hurrah!) and look for freestanding cabinets, chests of drawers and one-of-a-kind baskets to keep your clothes in.

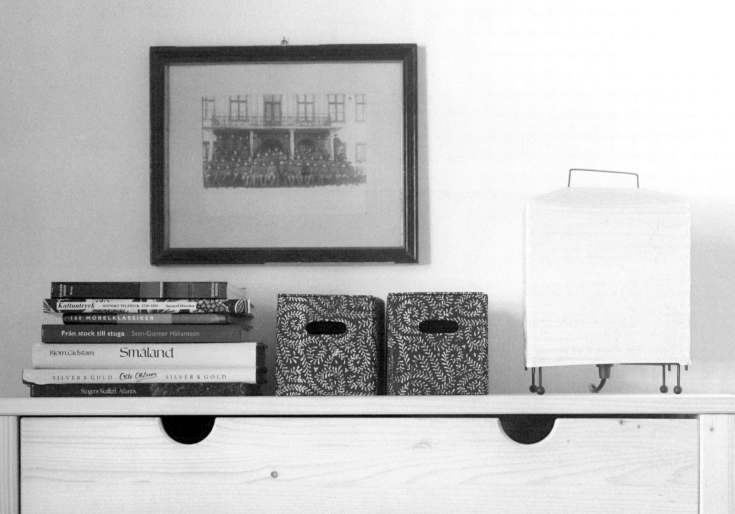

MOM, CAN WE HAVE PINK
WALLS - PLEASE? OF COURSE
YOU CAN! AND A RED FLOOR?
NO PROBLEM. AND A BED CANOPY?
ABSOLUTELY. CAN WE RIDE OUR
BICYCLES DOWN TO THE VILLAGE
AND BUY CANDY? NO!

the girls' room isn't that big, yet they still chose to put two pretty large day-beds opposite each other. only a chair fits in-between, but they've turned the lack of space into an excuse to create a fun, cozy little clubhouse. there's plenty of sisterly chitchat, goodnight talk and cozy moments when you're this close to each other.

54   Please take a seat — anywhere.

BYE–BYE FROM US IN HÖGHULT!

BELOVED
VÄSTRA BYVÄGEN

Out here in the middle of the southern Swedish countryside live

grandma and granddad with their cats and their nice white dog, Roxy.

This townhouse on two floors, with four rooms and a kitchen was built

in 1909, rebuilt in 1947 and completely revamped by this

couple in the new millennium. In the fine dining room this sweet old

couple like to have their dinner, enjoying life and listening to…

The Velvet Underground.

60   Nobody leaves the table! This couple chose plastic chairs with padded fabric cushions to make sure everyone stays at the table for a really long time.

61

Oops, what happened here?

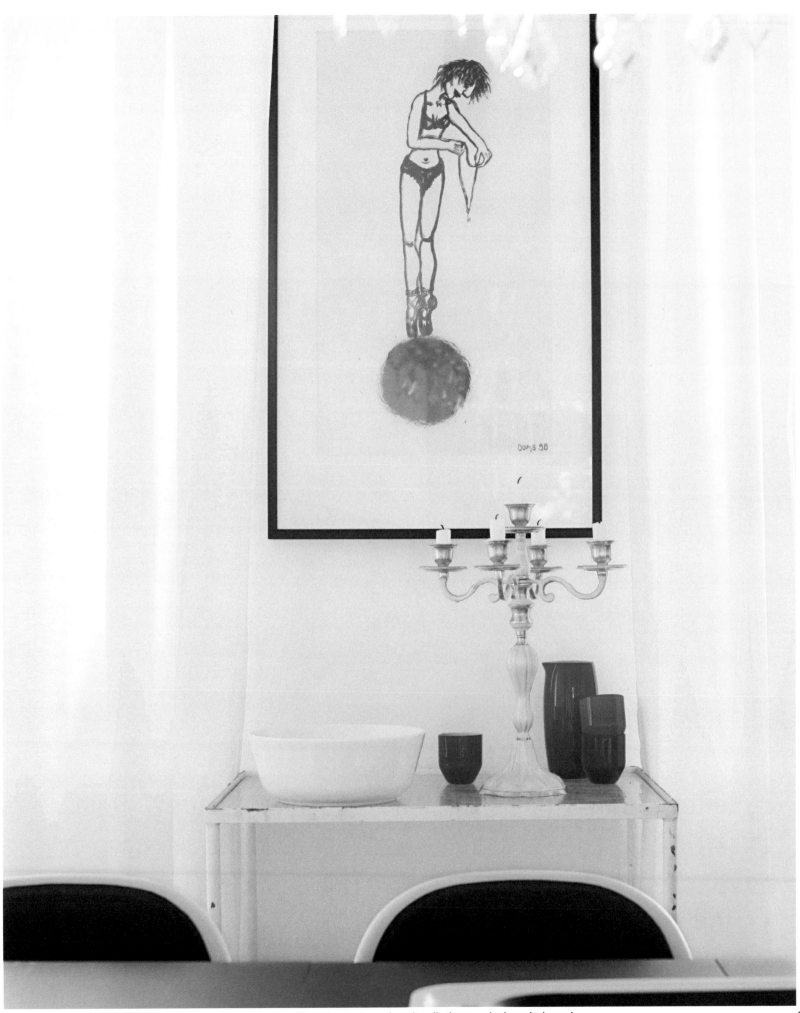

The service cart with candelabra had an entirely different purpose when it rolled around a hospital ward.

Rustic on the wild side.
The brick wall and the freestanding wooden kitchen give this room a rustic base. This way, the rest of the room can go a little wild with bright yellow, red, turquoise and stainless steel.

remember the hole from the previous page? here it is from the kitchen. making a hole in the wall gave them a link to the dining room. sledgehammer + idea = a brutal service hatch.
in the foreground, home-baked cake for rock fans.

We may be out in rural southern Sweden, but our couple has managed to create a kitchen that epitomizes Fifties America, with vinyl bar stools and a mini TV on the countertop. But the time is now. And the place is the very south of Sweden.

67

Cafeteria for cats.
The cats take their meals up on the
wood-burning stove to keep the dog from
devouring their food. The spices are in
the red metal bathroom cabinet.

Remember – only buy attractive food packaging if you have open storage in your kitchen!

A white leather sofa is super-cool and super-cozy in equal parts. Just ask Roxy (named after a rock club), who uses this room as a bedroom. Add some woolly stools, a soft rug and airy curtains, as our friends have done here, and the room becomes warm and comfortable without losing its edge.

white, white, white, white, fresh, fresh, fresh, and bright cerise.

Actually, everyone should have a bright cerise accent wall at some point in their lives.

The napping chair (complete with throw blanket) has good lighting in case reading interrupts sleep.

The result of boxing in a pipe became a kind of display surface in the living room, showing a collection of everything from genuine art to genuine junk.

this home perfectly reflects the couple that lives here. take a rough rock club and add a passion for interior design, and you have a beloved yet irreverent approach to what a home should look like. irreverent in the most positive sense of the word, of course. basically, it's rocky but it's cozy, both at the same time.

THE SHELVES ARE WEIGHED DOWN BY TREND MAGAZINES, PUNK LITERATURE AND PUNK MUSIC THAT'S HARD TO GET HOLD OF ANYMORE.

Advanced Storage, lesson 1:
Behind the fabric there's a custom clothes rail built into the staircase, and a narrow open shelf for knick-knacks.

Advanced Storage, lesson 2:
Under the stairs are some incredible wines in the perfect environment. Would you like a wine cellar too? Find an empty corner in the basement (could be the hardest part), take a piece of cardboard and a felt marker, and there you have it!

from the vestibule – with moss-green tile flooring and a bench with bamboo details – you can see all the way into the dining room. the stairs lead to the bedrooms upstairs. furthest in you can just see a stoneware pot for granddad's cane. oops! sorry! umbrella.

the upstairs isn't as spacious as the downstairs, and has less storage, so the key is to try to make the very most of all the space on hand. the sloping roof area in the bedroom is therefore used for clothes storage. and rather than standard wardrobe doors - which wouldn't fit - they've used a fabric drape as a door.

Simple, neat and restful, with light from the shower next door. But knowing our couple, that metal cabinet probably has CDs in it and not your run-of-the-mill bathroom things.

Pop Art, plastic stools and a plastic mat
make laundry time loads more fun.

BYE-BYE
FROM US
ON
VÄSTRA BYVÄGEN!

BELOVED
TRANVÄGEN

Lisa and Mattias live the city life in a meticulously

renovated, functionalist 1-bedroom apartment from the Thirties.

They work, pursue their careers and are enthusiastic, professional

and ambitious, as we all are (for a certain period in our lives

at least). So they're never home. But when they do come home,

they enjoy it totally. And they keep things in order, big time.

Come on in, but please, don't make a mess!

RELAX-FEST

A home doesn't have to be full of stuff to make it feel welcoming. This one-bedroom apartment exudes a sense of peace and quiet. Of neatness and tidiness. Of coolness and freshness. Just the kind of qualities you need when life outside the home is full of stress and excitement, noise and constant demands.

SOUVENIR-FREE ZONE

IF YOU'RE A THING, AND WANT TO BE SEEN,
YOU HAVE TO HAVE A VERY GOOD REASON WHY.
JUST LOOKING GOOD ISN'T ENOUGH.
THE THING HAS TO BE SMART,
AND HAVE AN INTERESTING STORY TO TELL.
THESE PEOPLE ACTUALLY HAVE A LOT OF
THINGS, BUT MOST ARE PUT AWAY.
IF IT IS VISIBLE, IT'S BEEN SELECTED WITH
THE UTMOST CARE. EVERYTHING ELSE
IS BEHIND CLOSED DOORS.

90   Twice as good. The table legs have a double function – legs + storage. Double table – room for Lisa + Mattias. Double storage – over + under.
Double function – top + storage.

um... we're not working...

oh no? then why the extra-long desk and two chairs along the living room wall? with adjacent workspaces at least they sit together when they work. under the glass table top are various things for different reasons. nice-looking. important. good to have close by. on the wall are plenty of cabinets with room for loads of stuff.

The brown or white fight.
Lisa had her mind set on a white kitchen.
Mattias wanted brown. He wanted to
create a contrast and draw the line
between work and home – because
almost all restaurant kitchens are white.
Lisa – who grew up in a brown Seventies
kitchen – refused. Separation? No, nothing
that dramatic! Discussion and excursion.
And on one look-at-kitchens outing they
spotted a kitchen that – incredibly – they
both liked. Warm brown doors in white
surroundings, without the smell of Lisa's
Seventies, and instead the fine aroma
of Mattias's cooking. Actually, because
Mattias is a chef by trade, the functionality
and practical aspects of the kitchen were
in fact much more important than the
color.

94   The island isn't a sit-at-and-eat island, but a work-in-the-kitchen island. They eat at the small dining table, which can actually seat four people for dinner.

To keep as much valuable floor space free as possible, they've chosen wall shelves rather than bedside tables. The reading lamps come from Lisa's parents' place.

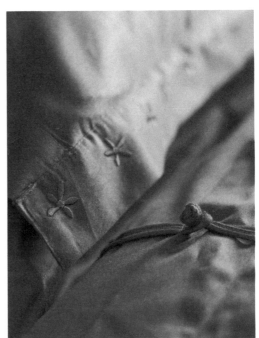

this room was too small for an ordinary wardrobe. and the need for closed storage was tremendous. think vertically and count in cubic feet instead of floor area! the result is a super-duper storage thingamajig that holds everything. and because it's only about 12 inches (30 cm) deep the room still feels pretty spacious. on the top are boxes for stuff you never need (and probably forgot you even have).

the bathroom may not be big, but it still has room for a small bathtub - on feet! and of course tons of storage.

how do you combine aesthetics, minimalism-
light and loads of jackets? by using the hall
very smartly. the best-looking garments are
on the hooks, while warm but ugly winter hats
go in the boxes on the shelf. open storage,
closed storage in the wardrobe, boxes, drawers
and small hooks. and although we can count
five different storage solutions from two
different eras, it still looks neat, spacious
and in line with the functionalist ideal.

BYE-BYE
FROM US
ON
TRANVÄGEN!

BELOVED
SÖDRA ALLÉN

An 18th century mansion. No one lives like this.

In fact the passionate owners of this incredible home don't live here either.

They are the house. They live and breathe their house.

This is where they have an outlet for their passion, their great interest in life:

renovating 18th century houses. At a leisurely pace they carefully

remove layers of paint, take a break to study their work, have a cup of coffee,

and do a bit more scraping. The guided tour starts now.

Please, come in!

Only two people live here. But because they live as they do, and are so infinitely hospitable, they're rarely without visitors. So however many guests turn up, there's always somewhere to put their coats.

if you have a lot of space – and this couple certainly does – you can make an attractive still life out of something as ordinary as a pile of towels.

Don't forget to lock both doors when nature calls!

112   The kitchen is about the size of a normal two-bedroom apartment. Because kitchen countertops hadn't been invented yet in the 1700s, this one's new. In fact the whole kitchen is new, but manages to blend in nicely with the rest of the room and the home. But of course not only

the furniture makes this home, above all it's the wonderful sense of symmetry. The positioning of the doors and windows. The balance that gives the rooms a feeling of restfulness, without really being able to say why.

once the first pangs of jealousy have passed, it's easier to enjoy the home's unique character with an exquisite blend of the new, the antique and the flea market bargain.

Nothing in this home is only for show, absolutely everything is used. Coffee is enjoyed from fragile 18th century cups without wrist-shaking nerves.

Talking about the living room and TV room seems like an understatement. Our couple lives in great halls – the TV hall, the living room hall, the bed hall, the reception hall, the bathroom hall, the kitchen hall, the reading hall, the hallway hall… you get the picture.

118   Living room hall 1. A more formal kind of relaxation in this room, with armchairs and soft sofas placed around a slightly higher coffee table.

Living room hall 2.
The TV hall is made to relax in. The couple can either doze off in a soft, cozy sofa, or an inviting chaise longue. Which is often what happens, since 21st century diversion usually means some half-boring light entertainment program on TV…
Modern reading lamps and the little serving cart blend in discreetly with the other furniture.

work from home? sure!

the work hall is probably one of the most beautiful rooms in the house - despite, or maybe because of, its diminutive size. simple furniture, stunning view, plenty of natural light from the garden, and even more light from all the nearby rooms in a row. relaxed and inviting!

Waste sorting 18th century style

instincts above the ordinary sometimes, the modern elements feel so natural that you barely notice them, as if there's no question that the count who lived here three hundred years ago owned a 21st century tubular steel table.

imagine being a grandchild in
this house. all that room to
run around in. the 18th century
mischief you could get into!

BYE-BYE FROM US ON SÖDRA ALLÉN!

BELOVED
BRUNNSGATAN

This home has everything mom Anna, dad John and

little Kalle, age 2, need. An overgrown garden with room for

coffee breaks and no-holds-barred outdoor fun,

a two-story brick house full of strong colors, some nice original

Fifties details and plenty of textiles.

So don't just stand there in the garden — come inside!

136   1,076 square feet (100 m²) over two floors is a lot if you keep it spacious. And space is exactly what Anna and John made the most of by taking away the wall between the kitchen and dining area. The dining area has an extra wide opening onto the living room and doors out to the garden.

THE HEART
OF HEARTS!

All that talk about the kitchen being the heart of the home. Not in this home! The kitchen island is the heart of this home. A table for breakfast and
buffets. A surface for folding laundry, sewing and drawing. A countertop for baking. This is where anything of importance happens in this family.

Long live the baby bottle! What are a few beautiful stones in a glass jar compared to this original still life?

Why only tile by the countertop when you can tile from floor to ceiling in the whole kitchen? Tiled floors, fully tiled walls and hardwearing stainless steel countertops make it easy to keep the kitchen clean, while black and white gives an austere impression.

Where's the brown sugar? Check the drawer. Where's the baby formula? Check the drawer. Where's grandma? Check the drawer. This kitchen can swallow anything.

clash more!
the sideboard is a fifties original,
and the chairs are real plastic.

Austerely smart. The black leather sofa is easy to keep clean and the coffee table is a bit higher than normal — the ideal height for little Kalle to play on. And the soft, red rug holds together the mix of textiles and materials.

146 When a full day's play is over, it's nice to be able to clear all the toys away. With four rooms including the kitchen, the toys are evenly distributed throughout all the rooms. So it's a good idea to have toy storage all over the place. Building blocks at the bottom, vases at the top.

FOUR SHOE HORNS, IS THAT REALLY NECESSARY? YES! ONE FOR SHOES. THREE AS SWORDS.

the perfect example of fifties functionalism. a narrow but useful hall with plenty of hooks on the hat rack. bring in a little 21st century ingenuity — child-height hooks, a chair for sitting and putting on shoes, and boxes on top of the hat rack for everything you don't need right away (but can never find if it's in the basement).

don't strip the charm away. here anna and john were brave enough
to keep the wild original wallpaper, and even enhanced the mixture
by adding more pattern and more color. the result is a charming,
extremely unique workspace. to make sure it didn't feel too dark,
they chose white workspace furniture. this upstairs space is used
to the maximum. in fact the whole house is. on 1,076 square feet
(100 m²) they managed to fit in a wonderful downstairs for
socializing, eating and playing, and an upstairs for sleeping,
working and taking baths. and outside there's that beautiful
garden for coffee-drinking and mischief-making.

REAL SOFTIE

KALLE MAY BE ONLY TWO, BUT HE
ALREADY HAS A BIG BED WITH ROOM FOR
A STORY-READING PARENT. AND THERE ISN'T
A HARD OBJECT IN SIGHT.
JUST PILLOWS, COVERS, SOFT RUGS,
COZY CURTAINS AND WARM COLORS, AS
WELL AS UNEXPECTED PATTERN COMBINATIONS.
AND BECAUSE THERE'S NO GUESTROOM,
KALLE GETS TO SLEEP BETWEEN
MOMMY AND DADDY (YEAH!)
WHEN GRANDMA'S VISITING.

The black color tones the room down a bit, but above all it brings out the very best in the fine headboard.

if the bathroom's a bit tight, which it is, it's a good idea to have a getting-ready space in the bedroom.

BYE-BYE FROM US ON BRUNNSGATAN!

BELOVED
KAPTENSGATAN

Here live three people – mom, dad, a teenager –

and a dog, all squeezed into 2,700 square feet (250 m^2). Squeezed?

Yes, squeezed is the word for it with all those wonderful artworks,

design classics, legendary LPs, must-have literature and 75,632 odds

and ends. At least. What record are you looking for?

Or was it a book? Aha, so you're only here for the art!

Well, please come in. Sorry it's so crowded…

DALA HORSE,
ANYONE?

The family likes to keep quite a tight
rein on all the collectables in the rest of
the house (right!). But here, the über-
collector himself has found his own little
nook which is called a study, but which
in reality is a collector's paradise. There is
some kind of creative method in all this
madness, in all the display cases, heaps,
boxes and cabinets. Apparently.

Imagine having so much space at home that you can devote an entire wonderful room to all the things you don't really know what to do with, but love so much you don't want to get rid of them. This is that kind of room. An all-my-wonderful-things room. A sit-back-and-enjoy room.

with this many books, you can't be so picky about where to put the library. the whole house holds some of the library, including the hall. but if the home's a little unconventional in the first place, then having books everywhere feels perfectly natural - and very, very homey.

Collection ref. 36: Fancy blue glassware mixed with glass from less than fancy bargain bins.

if you have plenty of room, like this family does, a dining room is a great place to be. it's so cool and calm. distinctly scandinavian. nothing crying out for your attention, but still an intimate, personal feel.

Chopin or heavy metal? Look around and you'll find both.

PUT THE GRAMOPHONE ON. DOES ANYONE STILL REMEMBER THE SENSE OF ANTICIPATION IN CAREFULLY LOWERING THE NEEDLE ONTO THE VINYL?

ON KAPTENSGATAN THEY DON'T ONLY REMEMBER IT, THEY LOVE PLAYING LPS ON FULL BLAST. THANKFULLY, STORAGE SOLUTIONS STILL EXIST FOR THESE MUCH-LOVED PIECES OF VINYL.

To counterbalance a compact black TV, they put it on a modern bentwood bench with soft, feminine curves.

where classics meet

the living room brings together design classics with new furniture and family heirlooms. because the color scheme is scandinavian light, it works well. the red and black add a bit of warmth to the scandinavian touch, which can sometimes be a bit cool.

ROOM FOR THE
HOUSE GUEST

The bed is in a recess, giving the impression of a special bed alcove — which helps create the feeling of a separate studio apartment. Nothing in this room has been chosen by mom or dad. Everything has been carefully selected with the most critical eye. A teenager's room is the first

step toward their own place (but without the rent or having to do their own laundry...). It really feels like a completely different home. A better one, of course.

the blend of modern patterns
and graceful lines is almost
symbolic in a teenager's room.
child or adult? both.

Different depths. Different widths. Different heights. A kitchen doesn't have to be perfectly straight to work perfectly well. And a kitchen on Kaptensgatan wouldn't be complete without a glimpse of some collection or other on top of the cabinets.

Make the most of every nook and cranny in the kitchen. Here there's room for everything: fridge and freezer, drawer unit on casters, shelving and a collection of cookbooks.

ONCE YOU HAVE A PANTRY YOU CAN NEVER GO BACK. WHERE ELSE WOULD YOU PUT ALL YOUR QUAINT JARS, FINE BASKETS, ORNATE CAKE TINS, CANDLES, LINEN AND PAPER NAPKINS, METAL TRAYS, DENTED SAUCEPANS, COOKBOOKS, WINE, WEIRD AND WONDERFUL PRESERVES, HUNGARIAN GHERKINS, FANTASTIC COLANDERS AND BIRTHDAY CANDLES? GOOD QUESTION.

BYE-BYE FROM US ON

KAPTENSGATAN!

BELOVED
BJÖRNGATAN

On the seventh floor, in a studio apartment with pantry kitchen lives Karin

— a fabric-maniac, a fabric-freak, a fabric-lover. She works with fabrics,

lives with fabrics and does interiors with fabrics.

She doesn't have that much space in her little fabric-packed pad, but she

has a lovely long balcony with a view of almost the whole city.

So if she ever gets tired of colors and patterns, she can always come

here for a breather. Ready for a fabric-fest?

Then step inside this cozy, functionalist studio apartment.

WHEN ARE YOU GOING TO HAVE TIME TO MAKE SOMETHING OUT OF ALL THAT?

NEVER! YOU DON'T HAVE TO MAKE SOMETHING JUST BECAUSE YOU LIKE

FABRICS. THEY'RE BEAUTIFUL JUST AS THEY ARE.

YOU CAN BUY FABRICS BY THE YARD JUST BECAUSE THEY LOOK GOOD,

OR HAVE A UNIQUE PATTERN. OR A FUN COLOR COMBINATION.

OR AN UNUSUAL COLOR COMBINATION. OR REMIND YOU OF YOUR GRANDDAD.

OR MAKE YOU HAPPY. IN FACT, YOU CAN BUY FABRIC BY THE YARD

HOWEVER YOU WANT, WHENEVER YOU WANT, WITH NO PLANS WHATSOEVER

TO MAKE ANYTHING OUT OF IT AT ALL.

All the furniture in Karin's home is white. Either painted white or white from the start. And why? Well, that's obvious – to put all the focus on the fabrics.

If you live in a small space you have to be particularly inventive. Okay, so I don't have a bedroom. Then, I'll get a bed that doubles as a bedroom. I'll have closed storage at the bottom, but so I don't have to hide all my papers, books, fabric samples and yarns, I'll put up shelves so all my useful things will look like one enormous still life.

you can get a heck of a lot into a studio apartment. the wardrobe?
under the bed. the library? up near the ceiling. the fabric store-
room? next to the bed. the shoe cabinet? right next to the wardrobe.

When the fabric part of the brain has had enough colors and patterns, where better to take a breather than the balcony?

the wallpaper is from the sixties, and despite its "unminimalist"
look it works with whatever cloth karin puts on the table. behind
the windowpane you can just spot the little red kitchen. her favorite
things are in glass-door cabinets to prevent them from collecting dust.

202   In the middle of the apartment is a perky little red kitchen. It's like a kind of glass box with sliding doors and maximized storage on the walls. True functionalism!

BYE-BYE FROM ME ON BJÖRNGATAN!

BELOVED
STENGATAN

Mia, Staffan and their three boys live in a townhouse from 1963.

The boys have about a hundred friends each. And this is where they gather.

And we can see why — the house is appealing with its light, smart

architecture. With this many kids around, you can either take the no-stay-

outside line, or the okay-come-in-but-don't-drink-juice-on-the-sofa line.

This family's chosen the latter. Do your parents know you're here?

Okay, come on in, hang your jacket up and go down to

the basement where the others are playing hockey.

OUTDATED BUT TOP-RATED!

cloakroom may sound a bit old-fashioned, but it's exactly what this family needs. the hall has to be able to swallow literally tons of clothes. bicycle helmets, hats, school bags, sports bags, handbags, backpacks, boots, cycling shoes… there's a shelf with hangers for the best coats, hooks for everyday use and a shelf for chucking hats on. there's also a three-tier shoe rack so you don't get that classic mountain of sneakers inside the door. the same storage-fest is repeated on the opposite wall.

210   Magic doors. Under the TV is a wall cabinet full of magic video game stuff. Open the cabinet doors and – ding-dong! – there's one of the
         neighbor's kids at the front door wanting to come in and play. If the sofa fills up with kids, there's always the rug, which is almost as soft.

FEW CLEAR RULES
= A SIMPLER FAMILY LIFE
HANG UP YOUR JACKET AND DON'T EAT
ON THE SOFA. TWO RELATIVELY SIMPLE
RULES MOST PEOPLE REMEMBER. CUPCAKES
AND JUICE, POTATO CHIPS AND LEMONADE,
SANDWICHES AND MILK = ALL SERVED AND
EATEN AT THE BIG HOBBY TABLE IN
THE RECESS BY THE KITCHEN.

Sometimes it can be completely calm and quiet even though there are 12 young boys in the gigantic sofa with a freestanding chaise longue. Have they fallen asleep in the middle of all the cozy cushions? More likely — they're playing video games.

211

212   Historic plant. The gigantic monstera next to the fireplace started out as a small cutting from Mia's parents' monstera, which they were given as a wedding present in 1960.

the hobby table is positioned in a light recess with lovely big windows so typical of sixties architecture. there are stackable stools around the table to make seating more spacious and less formal. if more people show up, there are extra stools over by the tv - disguised as tables. once the snack-crumbs have been wiped off, the table's used for sewing, fixing things, folding laundry... behind are boxes filled with things to do for adults and children alike.

Right next to the kitchen is the family study. Space is minimal, but it's used to the maximum. A sturdy table top runs along the whole wall, and as much wall storage is packed in as possible.

217

WILLE, 11.
LIKES PLAYING WITH:
SOCCER FIGURES.
WANTS TO PLAY: SOCCER.
WANTS TO BE: A SOCCER PRO.
WANTS: A FONDUE SET.

Each of the three boys has a small bedroom. The rooms — and the boys — are all different in character. The rooms are pretty small and have to fit a bed, clothes and their personal stuff. And for a boy, personal stuff equals quite a lot of stuff. Even so, good storage and strong colors keep the rooms looking relatively calm.

dare to not renovate!
when the bathroom already has
attractive sinks, original 1963
tiles and beautifully yellowed
pine with as many hooks as you'd
find at a sports club, renovation
seems pointless, if not total
madness. all this family needed
to add was a little stool.

this is probably the most peaceful room in the whole house.
tired parents of three children who have more than their share
of stuff to do, need a cool room with calming furnishings to
get their strength back.

Well, there should be five chairs around the kitchen table, but a certain little boy put his in the study next door.

Sometimes even the parents have friends over, but unlike the boys' friends, they don't usually rush down to the basement for a game of soccer. Instead, they wander into the dining room to study the extensive book collection before dinner.

232   Down here in the basement is a good old-fashioned recreation room, where many a soccer and ice hockey world cup is decided. Every day. Some of the world's soccer and ice hockey greats clash talents here, and the bench (or long sofa along the wall) is full of sports heroes. Good

thing the rug is nice and soft when you get tackled. There's also plenty of room if the guest heroes feel like a sleepover party.

THE TRUE HEART OF THE HOME

The kitchen is the natural gathering-place in many homes, but here – in a family that's crazy about bicycling – they prefer to get together as far in and as far down as possible, in a wonderful part of the basement called the workshop.

234

BYE-BYE FROM US ON STENGATAN!

238

Concept
Project Manager
Lena Allblom, IKEA Family Services AB
Creative Director
Christina Larsson, IKEA Services AB

Project Leader
Birgitta Hansson, IKEA Svenska Försäljnings AB

Interiors
Pia Kriisin and Johan Dalin, JOPIA

Photographer
Stellan Herner, Skarp Agent

Assistant Photographer
Maria Öhman

Text
Stina Holmberg, Rivercreek AB

Graphic Design
Elisabeth Björkbom, elisabeth björkbom design & concept ab

Illustrator
Klas Fahlén, Agent Bauer

North American Adaptation and Verbal Identity Consultant
Janet Colletti, Boco Text Studio/Boco AB

Translation
Comactiva Translations AB

Project Management and Production
Lill Forsman and Anki Hedberg, Bokbolaget AB

Repro
Fälth & Hässler AB, Värnamo 2007

Printing
Litopat S.p.A., Italy 2011

Paper
Insert: 130 g Scandia 2000, Lessebo
Cover: 240 g Invercote Creato matt

Fonts
Cablegram
Interface

Thanks to:
All the nine families
P-O, Calle, Robban and Xenia

© 2007 IKEA Family Services AB

ISBN 978-91-85727-15-5 English/American